2024 SOCIAL MEDIA CONTENT PLANNER & GUIDE

for Coaches, Consultants & Online Experts

Consistently Better Results

Louise McDonnell

Published by Orla Kelly Publishing.

Hi,

Thank you for choosing my planner! My commitment is that it will empower you to consistently create top-notch social media content for your posts and paid promotions. While I have a genuine passion for social media, my ultimate goal is to help you achieve exceptional results with minimal time investment. With over a decade of experience assisting businesses and nonprofit organizations in leveraging social media for marketing and sales, I've refined my approach.

Within the Sell On Social.Media Agency, my team effectively manages social media campaigns for businesses, while in the Sell On Social.Media Academy, I educate individuals on the precise actions required to attain measurable outcomes. I've distilled all of this expertise into the Planner to assist you in consistently delivering high-quality content week after week, aligning with your business or organizational objectives.

Visit www.SellOnSocial.Media/2024resources to access the following free resources:

- 2024 Social Media Content Planning Calendar (Value €159/£138/$159)
- Unlocking Social Media Success: 6 Strategies to Boost Leads for Coaches and Consultants: Free Training (Value€159/£138/$159)
- Building Your Bio Blueprint (Valued at €59/£50/$59),
- An invitation to join my private Facebook Group.

Let's connect on social media! You can find me at @sellonsocialm across all platforms. If you decide to share pictures of my planner, please remember to tag me and use the hashtag #Kickstart2024.

Once again, thank you for choosing my planner. I'm excited to be part of your social media journey in 2024 and beyond!

To your success,

Louise McDonnell
www.SellOnSocial.Media

Personal Details

Name:

Address:

Email:

In an Emergency Please Contact

Name:

Address:

Telephone:

Mobile:

Passwords

Brand Colours

Company Registration Number

Tax Reference Number

Vat Number

Tax Clearance Reference

Notes

CONTENTS

FREE
SOCIAL MEDIA
RESOURCES

Visit **www.SellOnSocial.Media/2024resources** where you can download the following free tools.

Free 2024 Social Media Content Planning Calendar
(Value €159/£138/$159)

This template is the exact one we use in our Agency to organize and communicate content with our clients. Download a 12-month planning calendar that will help you stay organized and on track. Within the planner, you'll also find the 400+ prompts featured in this book

Claim €377/£326/$377 of free online resources at www.SellOnSocial.Media/2024resource

www.SellOnSocial.Media/2024resources

Leveraging Social Media & AI: Strategies for Coaches & Consultants. Free Training

(Value €159/£138/$159)

Unlock the potential of social media and transform your business. Learn six time-tested strategies that will supercharge your lead-generation efforts. If you're a coach, consultant, or online expert looking to harness the power of social media to grow your client base, this training will take your business to new heights.

Building Your Bio Blueprint

(Value €59/£38/$59)

10 steps to follow to write a social media bio, which will help convert lookers into paying customers.

THE POTENTIAL OF SOCIAL MEDIA AS A LEAD GENERATION TOOL

In today's digital world, the internet has become an integral part of our daily lives. According to a report published by Ani Petrosyan in April 2023, a staggering 5.18 billion people worldwide, equivalent to 64.6 percent of the global population, were active internet users. However, what truly stands out is the fact that 4.8 billion individuals, or 59.9 percent of the world's population, were active on social media platforms.

These numbers highlight how much the internet is a part of our daily lives, mainly because smartphones are so common. Indeed, over two-thirds of the world's population carry a smartphone with them virtually 24/7. These compact devices reside in our handbags, rest in our pockets, and linger by our bedside tables, always within arm's reach.

For businesses seeking to connect with their ideal customers, this smartphone phenomenon represents an unprecedented opportunity. We know that our target audience is spending a significant portion of their online time on social media platforms. However, merely setting up a social media profile is no longer sufficient.

To harness the full potential of social media, businesses must embrace several key principles:

- **Consistency** In the ever-evolving world of social media, consistency is key. Regularly showing up on your chosen platforms keeps your brand fresh in the minds of your audience.
- **Authenticity** Authenticity builds trust. Share your genuine voice, values, and stories. Authentic content resonates with your audience on a deeper level.
- **Be Real** Share images, videos and content of you and your team. Faceless, generic social media accounts simply don't work.
- **Engagement** Being present isn't enough; engage actively with your audience. Respond to comments, answer questions, and create dialogues to strengthen connections.
- **Targeting** Know your ideal customer and their social media habits. Tailor your content to reach them where they hang out online.

SELLING SERVICES ON SOCIAL MEDIA: A UNIQUE APPROACH

Selling services online comes with its unique set of challenges compared to selling physical products. Here are some key differences and strategies to consider when marketing services on social media.

Firstly, services are intangible. Unlike products that you can touch and see, services are experienced and delivered in real-time. The person providing the service is integral to the experience. If the service delivery falls short, it directly affects how the service is perceived.

For instance, think about dining at an upmarket restaurant. Even if the food and ambiance are exceptional, poor service can ruin the overall experience.

In the digital age, where social media is a powerful marketing tool, service providers need to adapt their strategies.

1   **Position Yourself** Services are closely linked to the individuals offering them. Establish yourself as an expert in your field to build trust with potential clients.

2.   **Connect Personally** Social media is a great platform to connect with your audience on a personal level. Share your knowledge and stories that resonate with your target audience. The more people see your face and hear your voice, the more they will get to know, like and trust you.

3.   **Authenticity Matters** Authenticity builds trust. Be genuine and transparent in your online presence. Share your real experiences and insights to connect with your audience on a personal level.

4.   **Build an Email List** Email marketing is crucial for service providers. It allows you to maintain direct communication with your audience, keeping them engaged over time. Use social media to build your list. Remember you don't own your social media followers, but you own your list.

5.   **Lead Generation** Instead of using social media primarily for direct sales, see it as a tool for generating leads. Use it to attract potential clients and guide them through the sales process.

Establishing your Brand Narrative

Social media is a bustling platform with numerous brands competing for attention. Establishing your brand narrative is key to standing out and conveying to potential customers why they should choose you. Without a strong narrative, there's a risk of investing time and money in content creation and paid promotions without converting viewers into paying customers.

Your brand narrative is the heart and soul of your business, encapsulating its purpose, values, and unique identity. It's what sets you apart, resonates with your target audience, and forms a lasting connection.

Whether you're a startup looking to make a memorable entrance or an established business seeking to refresh your brand, this planner will be your trusted companion in shaping a narrative that stands the test of time and resonates with your audience.

To help you craft your brand narrative, answer the following questions.

What Is Your Business's Mission Statement?
Start with the basics. What is the primary purpose of your business, and what values does it uphold?

Who is your Ideal Customer?
Define your ideal customers. What are their demographics, interests, and pain points?

What pain/need does your customer have? What are their frustrations? What words or phrases do they use to describe their situation?

What are the end results you achieve for your customers? How are their lives better after having purchased your products/services?

List 5 benefits why your customers choose you. What can you say that your competitors cannot?

What are your core values?

Ask yourself and your team what principles and beliefs are most important to your business. What drives your decisions and actions? What do you stand for?

 **LouiseMcDowell**

What is your Brand Personality?

Gather your team for a brainstorming session. Encourage them to come up with a list of keywords or adjectives that describe how you want your brand to be perceived. Consider characteristics like innovative, trustworthy, friendly, or sophisticated.

Think about your brand as a person. If your brand were a person, how would they dress, speak, and act? Visualize their personality traits.

Brand personality traits are characteristics that help define and communicate a brand's unique identity. These traits guide how a brand is perceived by its target audience. Here is a list of common brand personality traits:

- **Authentic** Genuine, honest, and transparent in its actions and communications.
- **Innovative** Forward-thinking, creative, and willing to embrace new ideas and technologies.
- **Friendly** Approachable, warm, and welcoming, creating a sense of friendliness and camaraderie.
- **Professional** Reliable, trustworthy, and maintaining high standards of quality and expertise.
- **Youthful** Energetic, vibrant, and appealing to a younger demographic.
- **Mature** Established, experienced, and appealing to a more mature audience.
- **Casual** Informal, relaxed, and easygoing in its approach.
- **Formal** Dignified, traditional, and adhering to established protocols.
- **Playful** Fun, lighthearted, and known for its sense of humour.
- **Serious** Focused, no-nonsense, and dedicated to a serious purpose.
- **Sustainable** Committed to environmental and social responsibility and sustainability.
- **Luxurious** Associated with opulence, exclusivity, and premium quality.

- **Economical** Value-oriented, cost-conscious, and budget-friendly.
- **Adventurous** Bold, daring, and encouraging a spirit of exploration and adventure.
- **Nurturing** Caring, supportive, and focused on helping and nurturing others.
- **Empowering** Inspiring and motivating individuals to reach their full potential.
- **Reliable** Trustworthy, dependable, and consistent in delivering on promises.
- **Rebellious** Non-conformist, challenging the status quo, and pushing boundaries.
- **Sociable** Encourages social interaction, community, and togetherness.
- **Sophisticated** Elegant, refined, and associated with high culture and taste.
- **Caring** Compassionate, empathetic, and concerned about the well-being of others.
- **Pioneering** A trailblazer, innovative, and setting new industry standards.
- **Down-to-Earth** Approachable, unpretentious, and relatable.
- **Artistic** Creative, expressive, and appreciative of the arts.
- **Futuristic** Forward-looking, visionary, and focused on the future.
- **Rugged** Tough, durable, and suited for challenging environments.
- **Traditional** Rooted in history and heritage, respecting established customs.
- **Global** Inclusive, culturally diverse, and appealing to a worldwide audience.
- **Local** Focused on its local community and emphasizing local culture and values.
- **Clever** Intelligent, witty, and known for its clever solutions and ideas.

When defining a brand's personality, it's essential to select traits that align with the brand's mission, values, and target audience. The chosen personality traits help guide branding, marketing, and communication efforts, ensuring a consistent and resonant brand identity.

What Is Your Brand's Origin Story?

Why do you do what you do? What inspired its creation, and what challenges have you overcome?

What Are Your Brand's Goals and Aspirations?

Outline your short-term and long-term goals. Where do you envision your brand in the future?

What Emotions Do You Want to Evoke?

Describe the emotions you want your brand to elicit in customers. Do you aim to inspire, comfort, or excite?

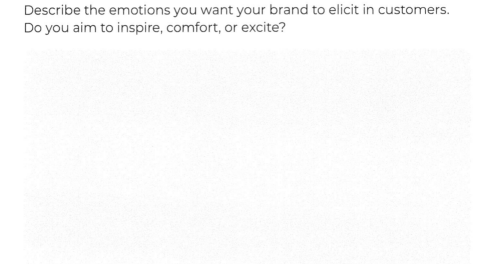

What Is Your Brand's Tone of Voice?

Define the tone your brand uses in communication. Is it formal, casual, humorous, or professional?

What Are Your Brand's Pain Points?
Acknowledge any weaknesses or challenges your brand faces. How are you addressing them?

What Are Your Brand's Successes?
Celebrate your achievements and milestones. What success stories can you share?

What Is Your Elevator Pitch?

Craft a concise statement that summarizes your brand's narrative and value proposition.

What Is Your Brand Narrative in Three Words?

Challenge yourself to distil your brand's essence into three words.

CONSISTENTLY BETTER CONTENT

Social media is about **connecting** with our audience and consistently communicating core messages to them.

The most important advice when it comes to creating social media content is this ...**it's not about what you want to say; it's about what your customer wants to hear from you.**

If you publish content that is useful to your customers, interests them, or ideally excites them, they are much more likely to engage.

When we publish posts on social media, we are reaching people at different stages of the customer journey. Some people will be more familiar with your brand than others. Some will be ready to purchase a product or service, while others will be earlier in their sales journey. For this reason, we need to produce different types of content to appeal to customers and potential customers as they move through our sales funnel.

I organise social media content under four pillars
- Brand Awareness
- Consideration
- Sales
- Advocate

Brand Awareness Content

Sometimes we are connecting

This is generally the best-performing content, as it's engaging, sociable content that your followers will interact with. It is less about selling and more about getting your brand in front of customers and potential customers. The aim here is to create brand impressions – how many times someone sees your logo, brand colours, etc.

The quality of your content and how much it appeals to your audience will determine their level of engagement (likes, comments, tagging friends, sharing). Keep it brief and use photos and visuals primarily; a picture is worth a thousand words!

Here are 65 ideas to get you started! Choose wisely; some of these ideas will work for you, while others may not. What is important is that the content you produce must be authentic to your brand. Top tip: Images and video thumbnails featuring real people generally reach twice as many people!

1   New Employee

Image of new employee.

For the post description include:

- Short text about the employee and their background
- Why they are excited to join the team
- Where they were before joining
- What they are most looking forward to

EX. "Let's extend a warm welcome to Mia! Mia, a recent graduate from NUIG with a master's degree in design, is 24 years old. Hailing from Kiltimagh in County Mayo, Mia is deeply passionate about sustainability and is a proud dog owner, cherishing her furry companion, Bambi."

2 New Partnership

Logos of new partnership for a graphic or a photo of the business owner.

- Text with the name of the partner and what they are going to bring to the table

EX. "We're thrilled to announce our partnership with @ Recyclestudios in Birmingham as we work toward our goal of creating a carbon-neutral environment in the coming years! Discover more at www.websitehere.com."

3 Partner Events/Opportunities

Event Image including logos of the partners within the event for a graphic.

- Text sharing the who, what, where, and when of the event or opportunities with your business/brand

EX. "Exciting news! We're teaming up with our friends at [Partner Business Name] to bring you an unforgettable event! 🌟 Join us for a night of [Event Theme] on [Event Date] at [Event Location]. Get ready for a memorable evening filled with [Highlight Key Activities or Attractions]. Stay tuned for more updates and surprises. Save the date and invite your friends - you won't want to miss this! #CollaborationEvent"

4 Day In The Life

A video would be best to show the routine of you and your business. A reel-style video featuring many short video clips and images would work well.

- Text about how you got started with your routine

EX. "Come along and be a business owner for a day with Carrie, our founder!"

5   Motivation/Quotes

Graphic with the motivational quote written out.

•   Why are you sharing this quote

•   Relate the quote in some way to a personal or business story

EX. (Quote about health) "Your health is your wealth and it's important to prioritise it! I remember well the day I got the worst news about..."

6   How I Got My Start
7   Donation Work
8   Company Mission
9   New Opportunities
10   Comparison
11   Go-To Tool Kit
12   Trending News Related To Your Industry /Niche
13   Company Values
14   Bumps In The Road That Bother You
15   Creators You Enjoy This Week
16   Ask For Viewers Best Advice
17   Employees In Action
18   Favourite Tools
19   Checklist
20   Anniversary Of Business
21   Favourite Books
22   Favourite Podcasts
23   Someone Who Inspires You
24   This Or That
25   New Talents
26   Bucket List
27   Story Behind Your Name Or Logo
28   Show Off Your Town/Location
29   How You Unwind After Work
30   Best Advice You Received
31   A Passion Of Yours Outside Your Business

Sometimes we are building authority

This type of content allows your customers to connect with your brand in a more meaningful way. Consideration posts, often referred to as expert content, offer advice or education. How can you assist your ideal customer right now? What advice can you provide? Think about positioning your company as an expert in the eyes of potential customers.

Here are 10 ideas for consideration content that you can incorporate into your content strategy. You can present this content as videos, reels, or multi-image swipe posts. This is strategic content that can leave a lasting impression on cold prospects, so consider allocating a budget to reach non-followers who match the profile of your ideal customer.

1   Top Tips

Could be a graphic with the words directly on the graphic or a short video (created in Canva or of you speaking to camera)

Use the post description to intrigue the viewer to watch the video. What can you say in the first line of the description to draw viewers in? Include a call to action such as "leave an emoji if you agree" or "share this with someone who needs to hear this."

EX. Here are 5 tips to keep your indoor plants flowering for longer......the last tip might surprise you... Have you any tips to add to this?

2   FAQ Answers

A short video answering a question that you often are asked about your business.

Remember to catch the attention of the viewer in the first few words of your post description.

EX. "People often inquire about strategies for achieving a better work-life balance. Here are three valuable tips that can help."

3   "How To" Tutorial

Short Video with a voiceover on how to do something that you would consider yourself an expert in.

Text should entice the viewers to watch the video the entire way through.

EX. Struggling with sleepless nights as a new parent? Check out this informative video where I share essential tips for getting your newborn into a healthy sleep routine. 👶 Discover the secrets to peaceful nights and happy mornings.

#NewbornSleep #ParentingTips #SweetDreams!

4   Ask Me Anything

Good as a story post with the use of the question button.

Short text on the story or stories preceding the Ask Me Anything post

EX. "Have nutrition questions? Ask the expert! 👩 Our Nutritionist Coach, [Coach's Name], is here to answer all your burning FAQs!

😟   Curious about portion control?

🌾 Wondering about gluten-free options?

🥤 Confused about hydration?

Drop your questions in the comments below ⬇️, and [Coach's Name] will provide you with the expert guidance you need for a healthier you! 💪 Don't miss out! #NutritionFAQ #AskTheExpert #HealthyLiving"

5   Common Mistakes Customers Make

Share images of physical, visible mistakes or create a graphic listing common product-related blunders. You can also stagger these posts over time, avoiding back-to-back uploads.

EX. New to the road? Avoid these top three common mistakes that learner drivers often make!

- Ignoring Blind Spots: Always check your blind spots before changing lanes or making a turn! Safety first! ✔

- Over-Speeding: Stick to the speed limits, and don't rush. It's better to arrive safely than not at all! 🕐🚫

- Nervous Braking: Gentle braking is the key! Avoid slamming on the brakes and maintain a smooth ride. 🎚️💧

Ready to become a confident driver? Leave these mistakes behind and hit the road with confidence! 🛣️💪 #DrivingTips #LearnerDriver #StaySafe

Conversion or Sales Content

Sometimes we are selling...

Sales posts focus on presenting and promoting your product (ebook, digital course etc,) or service. They should compel the reader to take action. A well-crafted sales post focuses on highlighting the key benefits that the product or service offers to potential customers. The key here is to make these benefits crystal clear, addressing how your offering can solve a problem or fulfil a need for your audience.

Additionally, every effective sales post should include one, and only one, clear call to action (CTA). This CTA serves as a guiding step for your audience, directing them on what to do next. Whether it's a 'Call Now,' 'Email Here,' or 'PM My Page,' the CTA should leave no room for confusion.

It's important to remember that if your sales post lacks clarity or leaves any room for uncertainty, potential customers are more likely to move on without making a purchase. So, be concise, persuasive, and straightforward in your sales posts to maximize your chances of converting viewers into satisfied customers.

Here are 12 ideas for sales posts which you can integrate into your content strategy.

1   New Products/Services

Images/Video of the products or tangibles of the services.

Include a short video displaying benefits of the new products / services. Include details of early bird offers, incentives, and bonuses.

EX. "Are you ready to have a well-behaved and cheerful pup? Our latest dog training program is here to make it possible! 🐕 ✨ Meet our star pupil, Daisy, showcasing her impressive new behaviours! Say goodbye to leash pulling and hello to a well-trained, obedient, and happy dog! 🐶🖤 Don't miss out on this opportunity. Sign up today and let's get started! 🐾👏

#DogTraining #HappyPuppy #NewBeginnings"

2   Free Lead Magnet

Image of the lead magnet (free ebook, recipe book, worksheet, guide, checklist etc. – something of value your ideal customer needs/ wants).

Ex. "Attention business owners and HR professionals! Tired of employee disputes disrupting your workplace? We've got you covered with our new eBook: "5 Proven Ways to Avoid Employee Disputes." Discover expert insights and strategies to foster a conflict-free, productive, and thriving work environment.

In this eBook, you'll learn:
- Effective communication techniques
- Conflict resolution strategies
- Proactive HR policies
- Team-building tips
- And more!

Don't let disputes hinder your company's success. Get your FREE copy now and pave the way for a harmonious workplace! 🙌💼 [Link to Download]

#HRConsulting #EmployeeRelations #WorkplaceHarmony

3   Sneak Peaks

Short video with "teaser" images to show parts of the new of your business or any new products / services.

EX. "Sneak Peek Alert: Discover Your Path to Wellness in 2024! 📓🌟

Ready to embark on a journey to a healthier, happier you? Get a sneak peek of our upcoming wellness diary designed to help you thrive in the new year! 📖

Inside this diary, you'll find:

🌞   Daily wellness tips

📝   Guided journaling prompts

🥗   Nutritious meal plans

🧘‍♀️ Mindfulness exercises

📅   Goal-setting strategies

Stay tuned for exclusive insights, a closer look, and a chance to grab your very own copy! Your path to wellness starts here. 🌿📓✨

#WellnessJourney #NewYearNewYou #SneakPeek

4   Black Friday

Graphic of Black Friday sales from your business accompanied by product images.

EX. "Black Friday Yoga Extravaganza! Save 70% Off 🌟🧘‍♂️

Ready to rejuvenate your mind, body, and soul from the comfort of your home? 🏡✨ This Black Friday, we're offering an exclusive 70% discount on our online yoga course!

🧘‍♀️ Dive into a world of serenity and wellness with:

☑️   Expert-led yoga sessions

🌿   Mindfulness practices

🍎   Nutritional guidance

📅   Flexible schedules

💬   Supportive community

Don't miss this opportunity to prioritize your well-being at an unbeatable price. Limited slots available, so grab your discount now! 🙏💻

#BlackFridayDeal #YogaJourney #SelfCareSale"

5   Christmas Gift Ideas

A single image, or a multi-image post or fast-moving video.

EX. Holiday Cheer for Menopause Wellness! Introducing Our Christmas Bundle! 🌟🎄Ladies, give yourself the gift of menopause comfort and vitality this Christmas! 🎁✨ Our special Christmas bundle is here, crafted with love to support you on your menopause journey.

Inside this festive package:

❄️ Expert menopause guides

🎁 Self-care goodies

🍵 Nourishing herbal teas

🧘 Exclusive access to online wellness sessions

'Tis the season to embrace menopause with confidence and joy. Don't miss out on this limited-time offer – unwrap the gift of well-being! 🧖‍♀️✨ [Link to Purchase]

#MenopauseWellness #ChristmasBundle #GiftOfSelfCare

Advocate Content

Sometimes we are impressing...

Advocate content, often generated by your most devoted customers and fans, holds immense value in the eyes of potential customers. It's a powerful asset, as people tend to place more trust in the opinions and experiences of others rather than just relying on your own claims.

To leverage this invaluable resource, consider implementing strategies to encourage and reward customers for sharing their reviews and recommendations. Make it easy for them to provide feedback on platforms like your Facebook page, LinkedIn Recommendations, Google Map Listing, or website. Create a seamless system that motivates as many customers as possible to leave reviews, ensuring a diverse range of voices.

Handpick individuals whom you know have had positive experiences and are likely to leave glowing reviews. Additionally, don't hesitate to ask some of your satisfied customers to share video reviews. These video testimonials can be used as standalone content to build trust or compiled into a compelling collage of authentic voices that sing your praises.

By harnessing advocate content and showcasing the genuine satisfaction of your clientele, you'll bolster your credibility and make a lasting impression on potential customers. Trust the power of real experiences and let your advocates be your best brand ambassadors!

Here are 13 ideas for advocate content that you can integrate into your content calendar.

1   Customer Success Stories

Image(s) of the customer with their success.

EX. "Real Transformation, Real Results! 🧠💪 Meet [Client's Name], a shining example of mental fitness success! 🧍 [Client's Name] embarked on a journey to enhance their mental well-being with our Mental Fitness Coaching Programme, and the results are truly remarkable. From conquering stress to boosting confidence, they've unlocked their full potential. 🚀🧠 Read their inspiring story and discover how you can transform your life too. 🔗✨ [Link to Client's Success Story]

Ready to rewrite your own success story? Let's embark on this journey together! 🌟🔑

#MentalFitness #SuccessStory #RealResults!"

2   Customer Testimonials

Photo or video of your customer or a graphic image with a quote from the customer.

Use the following formula: Greatest benefit to the client + the timeframe + how they feel now.

EX. I tripled my website sales after only three months of joining 'Sell on Social Media Academy'. I'm delighted." 🎉

Discover how you too can achieve remarkable results and turn your online business dreams into reality. Join us today! 📊🧍

#SuccessStory #OnlineSales #Delighted

3   On a Local Radio Station

Image of you at the radio station before or after an interview.

EX. "Don't forget to tune in to Star 101 FM to listen to my interview with @yourinterviewer. Thanks so much for having me, I had a blast! @theradioshow"

4   New Certification

Image of you with your new certification.

EX. "Officially certificated in Massage Therapy! We are beyond excited to add massages to our list of services and are looking forward to seeing you at the salon here soon to try it out! ✨✨✨"

5   Reposts of Features on Other Social Media Pages

Repost posts from other accounts that feature your business.

Great for a story post.

Text should be short and sweet, thanking the original poster and, if applicable, directing your audience to support them as well.

EX. "Shoutout to Amy Fowler for the awesome review and post of our products. We always enjoy your company and your business. Check out her page for some great updates on everything about small businesses! 🎉🙌"

6   Nomination for an Award

7   Winning an Award

8   Attending an Award Ceremony

9   New Qualification

10   Featured in Media

11   Influencer Post

12   Client Awards

13   Internal Company Promotions

How to Get Social Media Posts Seen by More People

How you present your posts on social media can significantly impact your reach. Social media platforms employ algorithms that govern content distribution. These algorithms favour content that garners engagement shortly after publication. Think of 'engagement'—likes, comments, views, clicks—as votes for your content.

Effective Social Media Post Descriptions

Your approach to crafting social media posts can significantly influence your reach. Social media platforms employ algorithms that dictate content distribution, favouring posts that quickly gather engagement—likes, comments, views, clicks—as votes for your content.

Consider this comprehensive checklist each time you create a post:

1 **Timing Matters** Carefully select the day and time to publish your post. Ensure your audience is present and has the time to engage by liking, commenting, sharing, clicking, or viewing.

2 **Visual Appeal** Utilize eye-catching graphics that capture attention while users scroll. Posts featuring real people from your company tend to perform exceptionally well.

3 **Variety is Key** Create diverse content, including short videos, single images, and carousel posts.

4 **Direct Links** Include direct product links or guide visitors on making a purchase. Simplify the buying decision.

5 **Use Links Sparingly** Reserve weblinks for necessary instances. Posting the link as a comment can enhance post performance.

6 **Mix Content** Diversify content categories, encompassing awareness, consideration, sales, and advocate content.

7 **Engaging Descriptions** Craft post descriptions with precision. The initial line must captivate readers and encourage them to read further. Share additional insights to enhance understanding.

8 **Clear CTA** Present one clear call to action to direct your audience's next step.

9 **Harness Hashtags** Amplify your reach with relevant hashtags.

10 **Strategic Tagging** Tag other relevant accounts, locations, and products. Opt for strategic tagging to capture attention, potentially leading to content sharing.

15 Call To Action Prompts to Include in Social Media Post Descriptions

1 Save this post for later

2 Share if you found this post useful

3 Drop an emoji if you agree

4 Click the link in bio...

5 Follow for more updates

6 Comment below and let me know your thoughts on...

7 Double tap if you agree

8 Hit (love heart sign) if you agree

9 Share this with someone who will benefit

10 Tag a friend

11 Swipe to learn more

12 Take a screenshot

13 DM me

14 Watch till the end

15 Repost to your story if...

Cracking the Code: 5 Key Factors Social Media Algorithms Consider

Social media algorithms are used by platforms like Facebook, Instagram, LinkedIn, and others to determine what content to show to users in their feeds.

1   Consistently appearing accounts are those that follow a regular posting schedule, maintain high-quality content, and overall messaging. These accounts prioritize consistency in their online presence, which contributes to their credibility, engagement, and audience retention.

2   Algorithms prioritize content that is likely to generate high engagement. Posts with more likes, comments, shares, and other forms of interaction are considered more engaging. Higher engagement indicates that the content is valuable and interesting to users.

3   Social media algorithms often prioritize trending topics, hashtags, or formats, giving them more exposure in users' feeds. This can help increase your visibility and reach beyond your existing followers. Following trends demonstrates that you are aware of and connected to current affairs, news, and events.

4   Algorithms take into account a user's past and present behaviour. This includes the types of content they have engaged with previously, the accounts they follow, and their interactions with specific users.

5   Stories have gained significant popularity across various social media platforms. Users that not only take advantage of their news feed but utilise their stories and highlights allow you to engage with your audience in a more informal and authentic manner. Use features like stickers, filters, location tags, and interactive elements (polls, quizzes, questions) to encourage viewer engagement and make your stories more interesting.

FOSTERING ENGAGEMENT: THE POWER OF TWO-WAY COMMUNICATION ON SOCIAL MEDIA

In the fast-paced world of social media, successful brands and businesses understand that it's not just about broadcasting messages to an audience; it's about creating meaningful conversations. Encouraging two-way communication is a crucial element of any effective social media strategy.

1. **Creating a Dialogue, Not a Monologue** Social media platforms are vibrant ecosystems where individuals, brands, and communities converge. It's a place for sharing, connecting, and engaging in conversations. To truly harness the power of social media, it's essential to shift your mindset from a one-sided monologue to a two-way dialogue.

2. **Empowering Your Followers** Your followers and customers are your most valuable assets on social media. They aren't just passive consumers of your content; they are active participants in your brand's story. Encourage them to share their thoughts, opinions, and ideas. Acknowledge their contributions and make them feel valued.

3. **Building Trust and Relationships** Trust is the foundation of any successful business, and social media provides a unique platform to build and nurture trust. When you engage in two-way communication, you're showing that you're not just interested in selling a product or service; you're genuinely interested in your audience's needs and concerns.

4. **Responding and Engaging** One of the most critical aspects of two-way communication is responsiveness. When your followers comment on your posts or ask questions, respond promptly and thoughtfully. Acknowledge their comments, whether they're positive or critical, with professionalism and courtesy. Engaging in constructive conversations, even when facing criticism, can enhance your brand's reputation.

5   **Showcasing Appreciation** Never underestimate the power of a simple "thank you." Expressing gratitude to your followers for their engagement can go a long way in strengthening your brand's relationship with its audience. Whether it's a heartfelt reply, a shoutout, or even giveaways to loyal followers, showing appreciation creates a positive and memorable impression.

The Benefits of Two-Way Communication

Engaging in two-way communication on social media offers several advantages for your brand:

1   **Enhanced Engagement** When followers feel heard and valued, they are more likely to interact with your content, share it, and remain loyal to your brand.

2   **Valuable Feedback** Two-way communication provides an invaluable source of feedback. You can gain insights into customer preferences, concerns, and ideas for improvement.

3   **Increased Brand Loyalty** Brands that actively engage with their audience tend to foster stronger relationships and, in turn, greater brand loyalty.

4   **Humanizing Your Brand** It humanizes your brand, making it relatable and approachable. People connect with people, not faceless entities.

5   **Crisis Management** In times of crisis or negative feedback, engaging in open and respectful conversations can help diffuse tension and resolve issues effectively.

6   **Algorithmic Rewards** Social media platforms' algorithms are designed to reward posts with higher engagement levels by giving them more significant reach. When your content sparks meaningful discussions and interactions, it's more likely to be shown to a broader audience. This increased visibility can lead to organic growth and expanded brand recognition, ultimately benefiting your brand's online presence.

AI POWERED SOCIAL MEDIA

What is AI?

Artificial Intelligence (AI) is a branch of computer science that aims to create machines that can simulate human intelligence processes, enabling them to perform tasks that typically require human intelligence, such as visual perception, speech recognition, decision-making, and language translation.

There are three primary branches of AI: regression, classification and generation.

Regression AI

Regression AI refers to the use of artificial intelligence techniques in regression analysis. Google Analytics is a good example of regression analysis AI. For years we have been reviewing our website's performance and using the data to inform future decisions on website content, ads campaigns, email marketing etc. Other examples include:

1   Predicting future sales based on historical data.

2   Estimating the risk in financial services.

3   Real estate prices prediction based on features like location, size, and number of rooms.

4   Predicting student scores based on attributes like attendance, hours of study, etc.

Classification AI

Classification AI refers to the use of artificial intelligence techniques to categorize data into predefined classes or labels. Examples of classification are all around us, but we probably didn't associate them with AI. For example, when Gmail classify emails as "spam" or "not spam" based on the content, sender, and other attributes of the email. Or when the image gallery in your smart phone has organised your images into categories by face recognition, or when financial institutions review a user's financial history and transaction details, an AI system can classify them as "creditworthy" or "not creditworthy".

Generation AI

Generative AI is a recent addition to the AI landscape. It's what has got us all fired up! With its ability to create images, sound, text, and videos, it's pioneering uncharted territories. It can produce entirely new content that didn't exist before, by learning patterns, structures, and characteristics from the training data. Examples include:

5   Text Generation: Models like ChatGPT or GPT-3 can craft entire articles, stories, or dialogues based on given prompts or continue a piece of text in a coherent manner.

6   Artwork and Design: Generative algorithms can produce new artwork or designs, sometimes blending styles or creating entirely novel concepts.

7   AI Videos: Generative AI models can produce realistic video footage of real people saying or doing things they never did.

8   Image Synthesis: Using tools like DALL·E from OpenAI, generative models can create unique images based on textual descriptions, like "a two-headed flamingo."

9   Music Creation: AI models like OpenAI's MuseNet can generate original music compositions in various styles based on given parameters or even mix styles of different composers.

The Benefits of Using AI for Social Media

- One of the greatest benefits of using AI is that it saves a huge amount of time. AI can help produce content quickly, whether it's crafting articles, creating visual aids for presentations, or generating other types of content relevant to their services.

- Using AI makes it easier to show up more consistently. To use social media effectively to generate leads, coaches and consultants must publish posts every week and spend time engaging with others. AI makes this easier to do.

- Using generative AI can position a coach or consultant as forward-thinking and technologically advanced, potentially appealing to a tech-savvy clientele.

- Generative AI models, when combined with other AI tools, can help in predicting trends or behaviors based on past data, aiding consultants, especially in areas like business strategy.

- In the long run, using AI to automate certain tasks can be more cost-effective than manual alternatives.

Concerns Associated with using AI for Coaches & Consultants

1. **Content Authenticity** If clients or followers feel that a coach's or consultant's content is mostly AI-generated, it may undermine the perceived value or authenticity of the content.

2. **Loss of Personal Touch** Over-reliance on AI could mean that a coach's or consultant's social media account has no real connection with the person behind the business. Remember, people do business with people they know like, and trust. It's important keep the personal touch, even if that means it's not always "perfect".

3. **Over-reliance** Dependence on AI tools can diminish a coach's or consultant's skills in manually handling social media interactions, making them overly dependent on technology.

10 Ways Coaches and Consultants Can Harness AI for Social Media Enhancement

1   Refining Bio/Summary and Profile Positioning AI can analyze successful profiles in the same niche and suggest improvements, ensuring that coaches and consultants present themselves optimally for their target audience.

2   **Brainstorming Content Ideas** AI tools can scan trending topics, competitor content, and audience interests to suggest fresh and relevant content themes and ideas.

3   **Crafting Social Media Posts** Leveraging AI, you can auto-generate engaging and optimized posts, ensuring consistent activity and outreach on platforms.

4   **Creating In-depth Blog Posts** AI can help draft detailed articles or blogs. With a topic in hand, these tools can provide a structured draft that consultants can then refine.

5   **Designing Lead Magnets:** AI can analyze what content resonates most with the target audience, guiding coaches in creating effective lead magnets like e-books, webinars, or checklists.

6   **Formulating Emails and Sequences** AI can tailor email content based on user behaviour and preferences, optimizing engagement and conversion rates for campaigns.

7   **Enhancing Ad Creatives** By analyzing high-performing ads, AI can guide the creation of compelling visuals and copy, boosting the efficacy of advertising campaigns.

8   **Boosting Community Engagement** AI-driven chatbots or automated response systems can facilitate timely interactions with followers or clients, ensuring they feel heard and valued.

9   **Facilitating Image and Video Production** AI tools can recommend visual content styles that resonate with the audience, and some advanced tools can even generate basic visuals or video clips.

10   **Gleaning Social Media Insights and Automation** AI analytics tools can provide deep insights into audience behaviour, preferences, and engagement metrics. Furthermore, AI can automate posting schedules, ensuring optimal reach and consistency.

AUGMENT ORGANIC REACH WITH PAID ADS

Paid advertising allows us to, not only reach more people; it also lets us control who we reach.

As organic (non-paid) reach is often sporadic in nature, we cannot depend on it to grow sales and generate leads. It is therefore essential, no matter what social media channel you use, to have a budget for paid ads.

Here's an interesting statistic...to generate 10 sales on your website, you must reach 25,000 people. This example is based on an average click-through rate of 2% on your posts/ad, and the same conversion rate on your website.

Obviously, you can aim for a much higher click-through and conversion rate, and this planner will help you achieve just that. The reason I have shared this example with you is that many business people have unrealistic expectations of using social media.

Reaching a few hundred or even a few thousand people with a post will not drive sales. The good news is that, if you use your budget wisely, and if your content/ads are of high quality, and of interest to your target audience, you can expect to achieve a high return on investment.

You are charged for ads based on how your audience responds to them. The more they respond the more people will see the ad. You set the budget but how that ad performs in down to your targeting, creative and messaging.

REVIEW PERFORMANCE TO INFORM FUTURE CAMPAIGNS

By tuning in to how our organic content and paid ads are working we can gain an understanding of what is working and appealing to our audience.

Here are some common metrics to note:

Reach — The number of people that saw your post or ad

Impressions — The number of times your post or ad was viewed. If one person saw your post/ad 10 times, that would be 10 impressions and one reach.

Engagement — The number of times someone interacted with your post or ad by liking/loving/reacting, commenting, clicking, viewing (if a video). (Engagement is directly linked to reach). The more people that engage, the more people your post will reach.

Clicks — Clicks on a post or ad.

For organic content tune into factors such as

- Time of day
- Days of week
- Media used
- Type of post (meme, product demo etc),
- Post description
- Hashtags
- Call to action

HOW TO MAXIMIZE THE BENEFITS OF YOUR CONTENT CALENDAR

Utilizing this social media content calendar effectively can significantly enhance your social media marketing strategy. Planning your content in advance offers several advantages:

1   **Reduced Stress and Enhanced Creativity** Planning ahead alleviates the pressure of last-minute content creation and allows you more time for creative thinking. This, in turn, can lead to more innovative and engaging posts.

2   **Time Savings** By dedicating specific time slots to plan and craft your social media content, you'll save valuable time in the long run. Consistency and quality content production become achievable.

3   **Inspiration from Prompts** Take advantage of the prompts provided in this calendar for inspiration. Tailor each prompt to align with your business's goals and values, ensuring that your posts remain relevant and purposeful.

4   **Diverse Content Opportunities** The prompts cover a wide range of topics, some of which can add a fun and light-hearted touch to your awareness content, while others can help position your business as an authority in your industry.

5   **Leverage Hashtags** Don't forget to incorporate relevant hashtags into your posts. This practice can increase the discoverability of your content by exposing it to users who follow those hashtags, expanding your reach beyond your current followers.

6   **Global Reach** These prompts are sourced from diverse locations worldwide, offering you the opportunity to connect with a global audience. This can be particularly advantageous if your business operates on an international scale or aims to expand its reach.

To make the most of your social media content calendar, establish a consistent routine for planning and creating content. Adapt the prompts to suit your brand's voice and messaging, ensuring that each post serves a specific purpose in your overall marketing strategy. By harnessing the power of this content calendar, you can enhance your social media presence, engage with your audience effectively, and achieve your marketing goals.

In addition to this powerful social media content calendar, there is a suite of invaluable resources that will supercharge your online presence. These free resources are designed to equip you with the tools and knowledge you need to thrive on social media:

Visit www.SellOnSocial.Media/2024resources to access the following free resources:

- **2024 Social Media Content Planning Calendar (Value €159/£138/$159)**
- **Unlocking Social Media Success: 6 Strategies to Boost Leads for Coaches and Consultants: Free Training (Value€159/£138/$159)**
- **Building Your Bio Blueprint (Valued at €59/£50/$59)**
- **An invitation to join my private Facebook Group**

These resources are your gateway to achieving remarkable results on social media. They are designed to complement your content calendar, helping you build a thriving online presence, foster engagement with your audience, and reach your marketing goals with confidence. Don't miss out on this opportunity to unlock your full social media potential!

Claim €377/£326/$377 of free online resources at www.SellOnSocial.Media/2024resources

2024
CONTENT
CALENDAR

 **Louise McDonnell**

JANUARY 2024

Date	Day	Date	Day
Mon 01	New Year's Day	Tue 16	Global Word Search Day
Tue 02	National Buffet Day	Wed 17	Intenational Mentoring Day
Wed 03	Festival of Sleep Day	Thur 18	National Thesaurus Day
Thur 04	National Trivia Day World Braille Day	Fri 19	National Popcorn Day
Fri 05	National Whipped Cream Day	Sat 20	National Penguin Day National Cheese Lovers Day
Sat 06	National Bean Day	Sun 21	National Hugging Day, World Religion Day
Sun 07	National Tempura Day	Mon 22	Celebration of Life Day
Mon 08	National Bubble Bath Day National Gluten-Free Day Clean Your Desk Day World Typing Day	Tue 23	National Handwriting Day
		Wed 24	National Compliment Day
Tue 09	National Apricot Day	Thur 25	National Irish Coffee Day Opposite Day
Wed 10	National Cut Your Energy Costs Day	Fri 26	National Spouses Day International Customs Day
Thur 11	National Human Trafficking Awareness Day	Sat 27	Holocaust Memorial Day
Fri 12	National Pharmacist Day	Sun 28	Data Privacy Day
Sat 13	National Sticker Day	Mon 29	National Puzzle Day
Sun 14	National Dress Up Your Pet Day	Tue 30	National Croissant Day
Mon 15	National Hat Day Martin Luther King Day	Wed 31	National Hot Chocolate Day

Sun	Mon	Tue	Wed	Thu	Fri	Sat
	01	02	03	04	05	06
07	08	09	10	11	12	13
14	15	16	17	18	19	20
21	22	23	24	25	26	27
28	29	30	31			

> Notes

 **LouiseMcDonnell**

FEBRUARY 2024

Date	Day
Thur 01	National Freedom Day
Fri 02	World Wetland's Day Groundhog Day
Sat 03	National Golden Retriever Day Icecream For Breakfast Day
Sun 04	World Cancer Day
Mon 05	World Nutella Day
Tue 06	National Lame Duck Day Safer Internet Day
Wed 07	National Send a Card to a Friend Day
Thur 08	National Kite Flying Day
Fri 09	National Pizza Day
Sat 10	Chinese New Year National Umbrella Day
Sun 11	World Day Of The Sick International Day of Women and Girls in Science
Mon 12	National Freedom To Marry Day International Epilepsy Day
Tue 13	Pancake Tuesday World Radio Day
Wed 14	Valentine's Day National Donor Day International Book Giving Day Ash Wednesday

Date	Day
Thurs 15	Singles Awareness Day International Childhood Cancer Day
Fri 16	National Almond Day
Sat 17	Random Acts of Kindness Day
Sun 18	National Drink Wine Day
Mon 19	Tug Of War Day Presidents Day
Tue 20	World Day of Social Justice Love Your Pet Day
Wed 21	International Mother Language Day
Thur 22	National Walking the Dog Day World Thinking Day
Fri 23	National Banana Bread Day
Sat 24	National Tortilla Chip Day
Sun 25	World Bookmark Day
Mon 26	National Pistachio Day
Tue 27	International Polar Bear Day
Wed 28	National Public Sleeping Day
Thurs 29	Rare Disease Day

Sun	Mon	Tue	Wed	Thu	Fri	Sat
				01	02	03
04	05	06	07	08	09	10
11	12	13	14	15	16	17
18	19	20	21	22	23	24
25	26	27	28	29		

> Notes

MARCH 2024

Date	Day		Date	Day
Fri 01	Self-Injury Awareness Day Zero Discrimination Day World Music Therapy Day Employee Appreciation Day National Day of Unplugging		Sat 16	National Panda Day
			Sun 17	Saint Patricks Day
			Mon 18	Global Recycling Day
Sat 02	National Old Stuff Day World Teen Mental Wellness Day		Tue 19	National Poultry Day World Social Work Day
Sun 03	World Wildlife Day World Hearing Day World Birth Defects Day		Wed 20	International Day of Happiness
			Thur 21	World Down Syndrome Day World Poetry Day
Mon 04	National Grammar Day World Obesity Day		Fri 22	World Water Day
Tue 05	National Absinthe Day		Sat 23	World Meteorological Day National Puppy Day Earth Hour
Wed 06	National Oreo Cookie Day		Sun 24	World Tuberculosis Day
Thur 07	National Be Heard Day World Plant Power Day		Mon 25	International Waffle Day
Fri 08	International Women's Day National Proofreading Day		Tue 26	National Spinach Day
Sat 09	National Get Over It Day		Wed 27	World Theatre Day
Sun 10	National Pack Your Lunch Day UK and Ireland Mother Day		Thur 28	World Piano Day Respect Your Cat Day
Mon 11	National Funeral Director and Mortician Day		Fri 29	National Mom and Pop Business Owners Day Good Friday
Tue 12	National Plant A Flower Day		Sat 30	Take a Walk in the Park Day National Doctors' Day
Wed 13	National Good Samaritan Day		Sun 31	National Crayon Day World Backup Day Easter Sunday
Thur 14	National Potato Chip Day International Day of Mathematics World Kidney Day			
Fri 15	World Consumer Rights Day World Sleep Day			

Sun	Mon	Tue	Wed	Thu	Fri	Sat
					01	02
03	04	05	06	07	08	09
10	11	12	13	14	15	16
17	18	19	20	21	22	23
24	25	26	27	28	29	30
31						

> Notes

APRIL 2024

Date	Day
Mon 01	April Fool's Day Easter Monday
Tue 02	World Autism Awareness Day International Children's Book Day
Wed 03	National Find a Rainbow Day National Walking Day
Thur 04	National School Librarian Day
Fri 05	Gold Star Spouses Day
Sat 06	International Day of Sport for Development and Peace National Handmade Day
Sun 07	World Health Day
Mon 08	National Zoo Lovers Day
Tue 09	National Unicorn Day
Wed 10	National Siblings Day World Homeopathy Day
Thur 11	National Pet Day
Fri 12	International Day of Human Space Flight
Sat 13	National Scrabble Day
Sun 14	National Dolphin Day International Moment of Laughter Day International Good Deeds Day
Mon 15	World Art Day

Date	Day
Tue 16	National Librarian Day National Wear Your Pyjamas to Work Day
Wed 17	No Limits for Deaf Children's Day
Thur 18	National Columnists Day International Amateur Radio Day
Fri 19	Congenital Diaphragmatic Hernia Action Day
Sat 20	National Lookalike Day Husband Appreciation Day
Sun 21	World Creativity and Innovation Day
Mon 22	Earth Day
Tue 23	National Picnic Day World Book Day English Language Day
Wed 24	National Skipping Day
Thur 25	World Penguin Day
Fri 26	International Chernobyl Disaster Rememberance Day World Intellectual Property Day
Sat 27	National Tell A Story Day
Sun 28	World Day for Safety and Health at Work National Pet Parents Day
Mon 29	International Dance Day
Tue 30	International Jazz Day Honesty Day

Sun	Mon	Tue	Wed	Thu	Fri	Sat
	01	02	03	04	05	06
07	08	09	10	11	12	13
14	15	16	17	18	19	20
21	22	23	24	25	26	27
28	29	30				

> Notes

MAY 2024

Date	Day
Wed 01	May Day School Principals' Day
Thur 02	International Harry Potter Day World Password Day
Fri 03	World Press Freedom Day
Sat 04	Star Wars Day
Sun 05	National Astronaut Day International Midwives Day —World Laughter Day —
Mon 06	National No Diet Day National Nurses Day
Tue 07	Beaufort Scale Day National Foster Care Day
Wed 08	World Red Cross Day National Student Nurse Day National Receptionists Day
Thur 09	Europe Day
Fri 10	National Clean Your Room Day
Sat 11	National Technology Day World Fair Trade Day
Sun 12	International Nurses Day US Mothers Day
Mon 13	International Hummus Day
Tue 14	Sex Differences in Health Awareness Day
Wed 15	International Day of Famillies
Thur 16	International Day of Light

Date	Day
Fri 17	World Telecommunication and Information Society Day Bike-to-Work Day National Endangered Species Day World Baking Day
Sat 18	International Museum Day Astronomy Day
Sun 19	Emergency Medical Services Day
Mon 20	World Bee Day
Tue 21	World Day For Cultural Diversity
Wed 22	International Day for Biological Diversity
Thur 23	World Turtle Day
Fri 24	National Brother's Day
Sat 25	National Wine Day National Missing Children's Day
Sun 26	National Paper Airplane Day
Mon 27	National Sunscreen Day Memorial Day
Tue 28	World Blood Cancer Day
Wed 29	Learn About Composting Day
Thur 30	World MS Day National Creativity Day
Fri 31	World No Tabacco Day National Smile Day

Sun	Mon	Tue	Wed	Thu	Fri	Sat
			01	02	03	04
05	06	07	08	09	10	11
12	13	14	15	16	17	18
19	20	21	22	23	24	25
26	27	28	29	30	31	

> Notes

Claim €377/£326/$377 of free online resources at www.SellOnSocial.Media/2024resources

JUNE 2024

Date	Day	Date	Day
Sat 01	Global Day of Parents	Sun 16	Fresh Veggies Day Fathers Day
Sun 02	National Cancer Survivors Day	Mon 17	Eat Your Vegetables Day
Mon 03	National Leave The Office Early Day National Egg Day World Bicycle Day	Tue 18	International Picnic Day
Tue 04	National Cognac Day	Wed 19	National Martini Day Juneteenth
Wed 05	World Environment Day Global Running Day	Thur 20	World Refugee Day
Thur 06	National Higher Education Day	Fri 21	World Music Day
Fri 07	World Food Safety Day	Sat 22	World Rainforest Day
Sat 08	World Oceans Day National Best Friend Day	Sun 23	United Nations Public Service Day
Sun 09	National Donald Duck Day	Mon 24	International Fairy Day
Mon 10	National Iced Tea Day	Tue 25	Global Beatles Day
Tue 11	National Corn On The Cob Day	Wed 26	National Beautician's Day
Wed 12	World Day Against Child Labour	Thur 27	National Sunglasses Day
Thur 13	International Albinism Awarness Day	Fri 28	National Insurance Awareness Day
Fri 14	World Blood Donor Day	Sat 29	National Camera Day
Sat 15	World Elder Abuse Awareness Day	Sun 30	Social Media Day

Sun	Mon	Tue	Wed	Thu	Fri	Sat
						01
02	03	04	05	06	07	08
09	10	11	12	13	14	15
16	17	18	19	20	21	22
23	24	25	26	27	28	29
30						

> Notes

 **LouiseMcDonnell**

JULY 2024

Date	Day	Date	Day
Mon 01	Canada Day	Wed 17	World Emoji Day / National Hot Dog Day
Tue 02	World UFO Day	Thur 18	Nelson Mandela International Day
Wed 03	International Plastic Bag Free Day	Fri 19	Daiquiri Day
Thur 04	Independence Day	Sat 20	National Moon Day
Fri 05	National Workaholics Day	Sun 21	National Junk Food Day
Sat 06	International Kissing Day	Mon 22	National Hammock Day
Sun 07	World Chocolate Day	Tue 23	National Gorgeous Grandma Day
Mon 08	National Video Game Day	Wed 24	National Tequila Day
Tue 09	National Sugar Cookie Day	Thur 25	National Wine And Cheese Day / Chili Dog Day / National Intern Day
Wed 10	National Pina Colada Day	Fri 26	Aunt And Uncle Day
Thur 11	World Population Day	Sat 27	Scotch Whisky Day
Fri 12	National Pecan Pie Day	Sun 28	National Milk Chocolate Day
Sat 13	National French Fry Day	Mon 29	National Lasagna Day
Sun 14	Bastille Day	Tue 30	National Cheesecake Day / International Friendship Day
Mon 15	World Youth Skills Day	Wed 31	National Avocado Day
Tue 16	World Snake Day		

Sun	Mon	Tue	Wed	Thu	Fri	Sat
	01	02	03	04	05	06
07	08	09	10	11	12	13
14	15	16	17	18	19	20
21	22	23	24	25	26	27
28	29	30	31			

> Notes

 Claim €377/£326/$377 of free online resources at www.SellOnSocial.Media/2024resources

AUGUST 2024

Date	Day	Date	Day
Thur 01	National Girlfriends Day World Lung Cancer Day	Sat 17	National Thrift Shop Day National Black Cat Appreciation Day World Honey Bee Day
Fri 02	National Colouring Book Day International Beer Day		
Sat 03	National Watermelon Day	Sun 18	National Fajita Day ational Couples Day
Sun 04	National Sisters Day	Mon 19	World Photography Day
Mon 05	National Oyster Day	Tue 20	National Radio Day World Mosquito Day
Tue 06	National Fresh Breath	Wed 21	National Finance Brokers Day
Wed 07	National Lighthouse Day	Thur 22	National Eat a Peach Day Burger Day
Thur 08	International Cat Day		
Fri 09	National Book Lovers Day	Fri 23	National Cuban Sandwich Day
Sat 10	National Lazy Day	Sat 24	National Waffles Day
Sun 11	National Son and Daughter Day	Sun 25	National Whiskey Sour Day
Mon 12	World Elephant Day International Youth Day	Mon 26	National Dog Day
		Tue 27	National Just Because Day Crab Soup Day
Tue 13	National Prosecco Day International Lefthanders Day		
Wed 14	National Social Security Day	Wed 28	National Red Wine Day
Thurs 15	National Relaxation Day	Thurs 29	National Chop Suey Day
Fri 16	National Rollercoaster Day National Tell A Joke Day	Fri 30	International Whale Shark Day
		Sat 31	We Love Memoirs Day World Distance Learning Day

Sun	Mon	Tue	Wed	Thu	Fri	Sat
				01	02	03
04	05	06	07	08	09	10
11	12	13	14	15	16	17
18	19	20	21	22	23	24
25	26	27	28	29	30	31

> Notes

 **LouiseMcDonnell**

 Claim €377/£326/$377 of free online resources at www.SellOnSocial.Media/2024resources

SEPTEMBER 2024

Date	Day	Date	Day
Sun 01	National Tofu Day	Wed 18	National Cheeseburger Day
Mon 02	World Coconut Day Labour Day	Thur 19	Talk Like a Pirate Day
Tue 03	National Skyscraper Day	Fri 20	National Pepperoni Pizza Day National Fried Rice Day
Wed 04	National Macadamia Nut Day	Sat 21	National Chai Day World Gratitude Day World Alzheimer's Day National Dance Day
Thur 05	International Day of Charity		
Fri 06	National Read a Book Day	Sun 22	Business Womens Day World Rhino Day
Sat 07	National Salami Day World Beard Day	Mon 23	International Day of Sign Languages
Sun 08	World Physiotherapy (PT) Day Worldwide Cystic Fibrosis Day	Tue 24	National Punctuation Day
Mon 09	International Sudoku Day	Wed 25	National Comic Book Day National Family Day
Tue 10	World Suicide Prevention Day	Thur 26	HR Professional Day World Maritime Day
Wed 11	National Hot Cross Bun Day		
Thur 12	National Video Games Day	Fri 27	National Chocolate Milk Day World Tourism Day Native American Day
Fri 13	International Chocolate Day Stand Up To Cancer Day	Sat 28	National Hunting and Fishing Day International Lace Day
Sat 14	National Cream Filled Donut Day		
Sun 15	Greenpeace Day	Sun 29	World Heart Day World Rivers Day
Mon 16	Working Parent Day		
Tue 17	International Country Music Day	Mon 30	Save The Koala Day

Sun	Mon	Tue	Wed	Thu	Fri	Sat
01	02	03	04	05	06	07
08	09	10	11	12	13	14
15	16	17	18	19	20	21
22	23	24	25	26	27	28
29	30					

> Notes

OCTOBER 2024

Date	Day		Date	Day
Tue 1	International Coffee Day International Music Day World Vegetarian Day		Tue 15	World Students Day
			Wed 16	World Food Day
Wed 2	International Day of Non-Violence World Financial Planning Day		Thur 17	International Day for the Eradication Of Poverty National Pasta Day
Thur 3	World Boyfriend Day		Fri 18	National No Beard Day
Fri 4	National Golf Lovers Day World Animal Day World Smile Day		Sat 19	International Gin & Tonic Day
			Sun 20	International Chefs Day International Sloth Day
Sat 5	World Teachers Day		Mon 21	National Apple Day
Sun 6	Grandparents Day National Physician Assistant Day		Tue 22	National Nut Day
Mon 7	National Bathtub Day World Architechture Day		Wed 23	International Snow Leopard Day
Tue 8	World Octopus Day		Thur 24	United Nations Day
Wed 9	National Emergency Nurses Day World Post Day Fire Prevention Day		Fri 25	World Pasta Day Frankenstein Friday
Thur 10	World Mental Health Day World Homeless Day		Sat 26	National Microneedling Day National Make a Difference Day
Fri 11	World Egg Day		Sun 27	National Mentoring Day
Sat 12	World Arthritis Day World Hospice and Palliative Care Day		Mon 28	National First Responders Day
			Tue 29	World Stroke Day
Sun 13	International Day for Disaster Risk Reduction		Wed 30	National Candy Corn Day
Mon 14	National Dessert Day Canadian Thanksgiving Columbus Day		Thur 31	Halloween National Magic Day

Sun	Mon	Tue	Wed	Thu	Fri	Sat
		01	02	03	04	05
06	07	08	09	10	11	12
13	14	15	16	17	18	19
20	21	22	23	24	25	26
27	28	29	30	31		

> Notes

 **LouiseMcDonnell**

NOVEMBER 2024

Date	Day
Fri 01	World Vegan Day
Sat 02	International Day to End Impunity for Crimes Against Journalists
Sun 03	National Sandwich Day
Mon 04	Nation Candy Day
Tue 05	National Love Your Red Hair Day
Wed 06	National Nachos Day National Stress Awareness Day
Thur 07	National Hug a Bear Day
Fri 08	National Cappuccino Day
Sat 09	World Freedom Day
Sun 10	National Vanilla Cupcake Day
Mon 11	Singles Day Veterans Day
Tue 12	World Pneumonia Day
Wed 13	World Kindness Day
Thur 14	World Diabetes Day
Fri 15	National Recycling Day

Date	Day
Sat 16	National Fast Food Day
Sun 17	National Homemade Bread Day
Mon 18	Mickey Mouse Day
Tue 19	International Mens Day Entrepreneurs Day
Wed 20	World Childrens Day
Thur 21	World Television Day
Fri 22	Go For a Ride Day
Sat 23	National Espresso Day
Sun 24	National Sardines Day
Mon 25	National Parfait Day
Tue 26	National Cake Day
Wed 27	Turtle Adoption Day
Thur 28	National French Toast Day Thanksgiving
Fri 29	Black Friday
Sat 30	National Mousse Day Small Business Saturday

Sun	Mon	Tue	Wed	Thu	Fri	Sat
					01	02
03	04	05	06	07	08	09
10	11	12	13	14	15	16
17	18	19	20	21	22	23
24	25	26	27	28	29	30

> Notes

DECEMBER 2024

Date	Day		Date	Day
Sun 01	World AIDS Day		Tue 17	National Maple Syrup Day
Mon 02	National Mutt Day		Wed 18	Bake Cookies Day
Tue 03	International Disability Day		Thur 19	National Hard Candy Day
Wed 04	National Cookie Day		Fri 20	National Sangria Day / National Ugly Christmas Sweater Day
Thur 05	International Ninja Day			
Fri 06	St. Nicholas Day		Sat 21	National Short Story Day
Sat 07	National Cotton Candy Day		Sun 22	National Cookie Exchange Day
Sun 08	National Brownie Day		Mon 23	National Roots Day
Mon 09	Anti-Corruption Day		Tue 24	National Eggnog Day
Tue 10	International Animal Rights Day		Wed 25	Christmas Day
Wed 11	International Mountain Day		Thur 26	National Candy Cane Day / Boxing Day
Thur 12	Gingerbread House Day		Fri 27	Visit The Zoo Day
Fri 13	National Cocoa Day		Sat 28	National Call a Friend Day
Sat 14	Monkey Day		Sun 29	Tick Tock Day
Sun 15	National Cupcake Day		Mon 30	National Bacon Day
Mon 16	National Chocolate Covered Anything Day		Tue 31	New Year's Eve / National Champagne Day

Sun	Mon	Tue	Wed	Thu	Fri	Sat
01	02	03	04	05	06	07
08	09	10	11	12	13	14
15	16	17	18	19	20	21
22	23	24	25	26	27	28
29	30	31				

> Notes

JANUARY 2024

> Monday 01

IRE, UK, US - New Year's Day

> Tuesday 02

> Wednesday 03

WEEK 1

> Thursday 04

> Friday 05

> Saturday 06

> Sunday 07

JANUARY 2024

> Monday 08

> Tuesday 09

> Wednesday 10

WEEK 2

> Thursday 11

> Friday 12

> Saturday 13

> Sunday 14

JANUARY 2024

> Monday 15

US - Martin Luther King Jr. Day

> Tuesday 16

> Wednesday 17

WEEK 3

> Thursday 18

> Friday 19

> Saturday 20

> Sunday 21

JANUARY 2024

> Monday 22

> Tuesday 23

> Wednesday 24

WEEK 4

> Thursday 25

> Friday 26

> Saturday 27

> Sunday 28

JANUARY / FEBRUARY 2024

> Monday 29 January

> Tuesday 30

> Wednesday 31

WEEK 5

> Thursday 01 February

> Friday 02

> Saturday 03

> Sunday 04

FEBRUARY 2024

> Monday 05

IRE - Bank Holiday

> Tuesday 06

> Wednesday 07

WEEK 6

> Thursday 08

> Friday 09

> Saturday 10

> Sunday 11

FEBRUARY 2024

> Monday 12

> Tuesday 13

> Wednesday 14

WEEK 7

> Thursday 15

> Friday 16

> Saturday 17

> Sunday 18

FEBRUARY 2024

> Monday 19

US - President's Day

> Tuesday 20

> Wednesday 21

WEEK 8

> Thursday 22

> Friday 23

> Saturday 24

> Sunday 25

 **LouiseMcDonnell**

FEBRUARY / MARCH 2024

> Monday 26 February

> Tuesday 27

> Wednesday 28

WEEK 9

> Thursday 29

> Friday 01 March

> Saturday 02

> Sunday 03

MARCH 2024

> Monday 04

> Tuesday 05

> Wednesday 06

WEEK 10

> Thursday 07

> Friday 08

> Saturday 09

> Sunday 10

MARCH 2024

> Monday 11

> Tuesday 12

> Wednesday 13

WEEK 11

> Thursday 14

> Friday 15

> Saturday 16

> Sunday 17

MARCH 2024

> Monday 18

IRE - Bank Holiday

> Tuesday 19

> Wednesday 20

WEEK 12

> Thursday 21

> Friday 22

> Saturday 23

> Sunday 24

MARCH

> Monday 25

> Tuesday 26

> Wednesday 27

WEEK 13

> Thursday 28

> Friday 29

UK - Good Friday

> Saturday 30

> Sunday 31

APRIL 2024

> Monday 01

IRE, UK - Bank Holiday

> Tuesday 02

> Wednesday 03

WEEK 14

> Thursday 04

> Friday 05

> Saturday 06

> Sunday 07

APRIL 2024

> Monday 08

> Tuesday 09

> Wednesday 10

WEEK 15

> Thursday 11

> Friday 12

> Saturday 13

> Sunday 14

APRIL 2024

> Monday 15

> Tuesday 16

> Wednesday 17

WEEK 16

> Thursday 18

> Friday 19

> Saturday 20

> Sunday 21

APRIL 2024

> Monday 22

> Tuesday 23

> Wednesday 24

WEEK 17

> Thursday 25

> Friday 26

> Saturday 27

> Sunday 28

APRIL / MAY 2024

> Monday 29 April

> Tuesday 30

> Wednesday 01 May

WEEK 18

> Thursday 02

> Friday 03

> Saturday 04

> Sunday 05

MAY 2024

> ## Monday 06

IRE, UK - Bank Holiday

> ## Tuesday 07

> ## Wednesday 08

WEEK 19

> Thursday 09

> Friday 10

> Saturday 11

> Sunday 12

MAY 2024

> Monday 13

> Tuesday 14

> Wednesday 15

WEEK 20

> **Thursday 16**

> **Friday 17**

> Saturday 18

> Sunday 19

MAY 2024

> Monday 20

> Tuesday 21

> Wednesday 22

WEEK 21

> Thursday 23

> Friday 24

> Saturday 25

> Sunday 26

MAY / JUNE 2024

> Monday 27 May

UK - Bank Holiday / US - Memorial Day

> Tuesday 28

> Wednesday 29

WEEK 22

> Thursday 30

> Friday 31

> Saturday 01 June

> Sunday 02

JUNE 2024

> ## Monday 03

IRE - Bank Holiday

> ## Tuesday 04

> ## Wednesday 05

WEEK 23

> Thursday 06

> Friday 07

> Saturday 08

> Sunday 09

JUNE 2024

> Monday 10

> Tuesday 11

> Wednesday 12

WEEK 24

> Thursday 13

> Friday 14

> Saturday 15

> Sunday 16

JUNE 2024

> Monday 17

> Tuesday 18

> Wednesday 19

US - Bank Holiday

WEEK 25

> Thursday 20

> Friday 21

> Saturday 22

> Sunday 23

JUNE 2024

> Monday 24

> Tuesday 25

> Wednesday 26

WEEK 26

> Thursday 27

> Friday 28

> Saturday 29

> Sunday 30

JULY 2024

> Monday 01 July

> Tuesday 02

> Wednesday 03

WEEK 27

> Thursday 04

US - Independence Day

> Friday 05

> Saturday 06

> Sunday 07

JULY 2024

> Monday 08

> Tuesday 09

> Wednesday 10

WEEK 28

> **Thursday 11**

> **Friday 12**

> Saturday 13

> Sunday 14

JULY 2024

> Monday 15

> Tuesday 16

> Wednesday 17

WEEK 29

> **Thursday 18**

> **Friday 19**

> Saturday 20

> Sunday 21

JULY 2024

> Monday 22

> Tuesday 23

> Wednesday 24

WEEK 30

> Thursday 25

> Friday 26

> Saturday 27

> Sunday 28

JULY / AUGUST 2024

> Monday 29 July

> Tuesday 30

> Wednesday 31

WEEK 31

> Thursday 01 August

> Friday 02

> Saturday 03

> Sunday 04

AUGUST 2024

> Monday 05

IRE - August Bank Holiday

> Tuesday 06

> Wednesday 07

WEEK 32

> Thursday 08

> Friday 09

> Saturday 10

> Sunday 11

AUGUST 2024

> Monday 12

> Tuesday 13

> Wednesday 14

WEEK 33

> Thursday 15

> Friday 16

> Saturday 17

> Sunday 18

AUGUST 2024

> Monday 19

> Tuesday 20

> Wednesday 21

WEEK 34

> Thursday 22

> Friday 23

> Saturday 24

> Sunday 25

 **LouiseMcDonell**

AUGUST / SEPTEMBER 2024

> Monday 26 August

UK - Bank Holiday

> Tuesday 27

> Wednesday 28

WEEK 35

> Thursday 29

> Friday 30

> Saturday 31

> Sunday 01 September

SEPTEMBER 2024

> Monday 02

US - Labor Day

> Tuesday 03

> Wednesday 04

WEEK 36

> Thursday 05

> Friday 06

> Saturday 07

> Sunday 08

SEPTEMBER 2024

> Monday 09

> Tuesday 10

> Wednesday 11

WEEK 37

> **Thursday 12**

> **Friday 13**

> Saturday 14

> Sunday 15

SEPTEMBER 2024

> Monday 16

> Tuesday 17

> Wednesday 18

WEEK 38

> Thursday 19

> Friday 20

> Saturday 21

> Sunday 22

SEPTEMBER

> Monday 23

> Tuesday 24

> Wednesday 25

WEEK 39

> Thursday 26

> Friday 27

> Saturday 28

> Sunday 29

SEPTEMBER / OCTOBER 2024

> Monday 30

> Tuesday 01 October

> Wednesday 02

WEEK 40

> Thursday 03

> Friday 04

> Saturday 05

> Sunday 06

OCTOBER 2024

> Monday 07

> Tuesday 08

> Wednesday 09

WEEK 41

> Thursday 10

> Friday 11

> Saturday 12

> Sunday 13

OCTOBER 2024

> Monday 14

> Tuesday 15

> Wednesday 16

WEEK 42

> Thursday 17

> Friday 18

> Saturday 19

> Sunday 20

OCTOBER 2024

> Monday 21

> Tuesday 22

> Wednesday 23

WEEK 43

> **Thursday 24**

> **Friday 25**

> Saturday 26

> Sunday 27

 **Louise McDonnell**

OCTOBER / NOVEMBER 2024

> ## Monday 28

IRE - Bank Holiday

> ## Tuesday 29

> ## Wednesday 30

WEEK 44

> Thursday 31

> Friday 01 November

> Saturday 02

> Sunday 03

NOVEMBER 2024

> Monday 04

> Tuesday 05

> Wednesday 06

WEEK 45

> Thursday 07

> Friday 08

> Saturday 09

> Sunday 10

LouiseMcDonnell

NOVEMBER 2024

> Monday 11

US - Veterans Day

> Tuesday 12

> Wednesday 13

WEEK 46

> Thursday 14

> Friday 15

> Saturday 16

> Sunday 17

NOVEMBER 2024

> Monday 18

> Tuesday 19

> Wednesday 20

WEEK 47

> Thursday 21

> Friday 22

> Saturday 23

> Sunday 24

NOVEMBER / DECEMBER 2024

> Monday 25 November

> Tuesday 26

> Wednesday 27

WEEK 48

> Thursday 28

US - Thanksgiving

> Friday 29

> Saturday 30

> Sunday 01

DECEMBER 2024

> Monday 02

> Tuesday 03

> Wednesday 04

WEEK 49

> Thursday 05

> Friday 06

> Saturday 07

> Sunday 08

DECEMBER 2024

> Monday 09

> Tuesday 10

> Wednesday 11

WEEK 50

> **Thursday 12**

> **Friday 13**

> Saturday 14

> Sunday 15

 **LouiseMcDonnell**

DECEMBER 2024

> Monday 16

> Tuesday 17

> Wednesday 18

WEEK 51

> Thursday 19

> Friday 20

> Saturday 21

> Sunday 22

DECEMBER 2024

> Monday 23

> Tuesday 24

> Wednesday 25

IRE - Christmas Day / UK - Christmas Day / US - Christmas Day

WEEK 52

> Thursday 26

IRE - St Stephen's Day / UK - Boxing Day

> Friday 27

> Saturday 28

> Sunday 29

DECEMBER 2024

> Monday 30 December

> Tuesday 31

> Wednesday 01 January 2025

WEEK 1

> Thursday 02

> Friday 03

> Saturday 04

> Sunday 05